Pop It in the Pan

and

Go, Ken, Go!

PHASE 2

/ck/e/

Level 2 – Red

Helpful Hints for Reading at Home

The graphemes (written letters) and phonemes (units of sound) used throughout this series are aligned with Letters and Sounds. This offers a consistent approach to learning whether reading at home or in the classroom.

HERE IS A LIST OF PHONEMES FOR THIS PHASE OF LEARNING. AN EXAMPLE OF THE PRONUNCIATION CAN BE FOUND IN BRACKETS.

Phase 2			
s (sat)	a (cat)	t (tap)	p (tap)
i (pin)	n (net)	m (man)	d (dog)
g (go)	o (sock)	c (cat)	k (kin)
ck (sack)	e (elf)	u (up)	r (rabbit)
h (hut)	b (ball)	f (fish)	ff (off)
l (lip)	ll (ball)	ss (hiss)	

HERE ARE SOME WORDS WHICH YOUR CHILD MAY FIND TRICKY.

Phase 2 Tricky Words			
the	to	I	no
go	into		

TOP TIPS FOR HELPING YOUR CHILD TO READ:

• Allow children time to break down unfamiliar words into units of sound and then encourage children to string these sounds together to create the word.

• Encourage your child to point out any focus phonics when they are used.

• Read through the book more than once to grow confidence.

• Ask simple questions about the text to assess understanding.

• Encourage children to use illustrations as prompts.

PHASE 2 /ck/e/

This book focuses on the phonemes /ck/ and /e/ and is a red level 2 book band.

Pop It in the Sack

and

Go, Ken, Go!

Written by
Robin Twiddy

Illustrated by
Amy Li

Can you say this sound and draw it with your finger?

Pop It in the Sack

Written by
Robin Twiddy

Illustrated by
Amy Li

It is Den. Den is a dog.

Get the sack, Den.

Den, go get the tack.

Pop it in the sack, Den.

Den, go get the pen.

Pop it in the sack, Den.

Den, go get the top.

Pop it in the sack, Den.

Den, go get the peg.

Pop it in the sack, Den.

Get in the sack, Den.

Den is in the sack.

Can you say this sound and draw it with your finger?

Go, Ken, Go!

Written by
Robin Twiddy

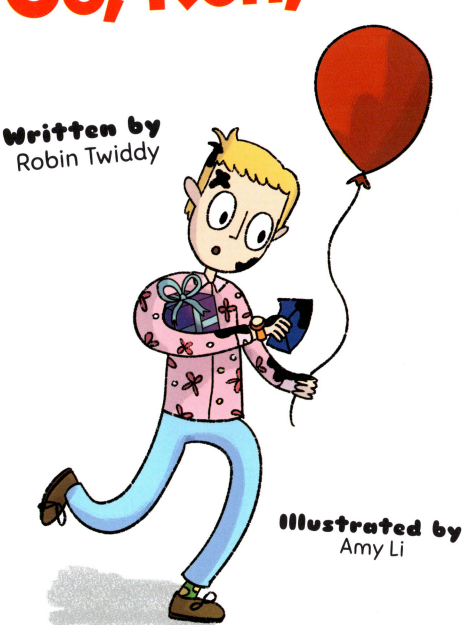

Illustrated by
Amy Li

Ken is on the go!

Get the sock, Ken! Tick tock.

No pen! Get a pen, Ken.

Tick tock. Tick tock! Go, Ken, go!

Dip the pen, Ken! Do not tip...

... the pot! Tick tock. Tick Tock.

Tick tock, tick tock.
Go, Ken, go!

Ken is in the pit. Tick Tock.

Go, Ken, go! Tick tock, tick tock.

Not the pin! POP! Tick tock, Ken!

Tap, tap. Tick tock. Tap, tap.

Ken is sad. Meg is not mad.

©2022 **BookLife Publishing Ltd.**
King's Lynn, Norfolk, PE30 4LS, UK

ISBN 978-1-80155-800-6

All rights reserved. Printed in Poland.
A catalogue record for this book is available from
the British Library.

Pop It in the Sack and Go, Ken, Go!
Written by Robin Twiddy
Illustrated by Amy Li

An Introduction to BookLife Readers...

Our Readers have been specifically created in line with the London Institute of Education's approach to book banding and are phonetically decodable and ordered to support each phase of Letters and Sounds.

Each book has been created to provide the best possible reading and learning experience. Our aim is to share our love of books with children, providing both emerging readers and prolific page-turners with beautiful books that are guaranteed to provoke interest and learning, regardless of ability.

BOOK BAND GRADED using the Institute of Education's approach to levelling.

PHONETICALLY DECODABLE supporting each phase of Letters and Sounds.

EXERCISES AND QUESTIONS to offer reinforcement and to ascertain comprehension.

BEAUTIFULLY ILLUSTRATED to inspire and provoke engagement, providing a variety of styles for the reader to enjoy whilst reading through the series.

AUTHOR INSIGHT:
ROBIN TWIDDY

Robin Twiddy is one of BookLife Publishing's most creative and prolific editorial talents, who imbues all his copy with a sense of adventure and energy. Robin's Cambridge-based first class honours degree in psychosocial studies offers a unique viewpoint on factual information and allows him to relay information in a manner that readers of any age are guaranteed to retain. He also holds a certificate in Teaching in the Lifelong Sector, and a postgraduate certificate in Consumer Psychology.

A father of two, Robin has written many titles for BookLife and specialises in conceptual, role-playing narratives which promote interaction with the reader and inspire even the most reluctant of readers to fully engage with his books.

PHASE 2
/ck/e/

This book focuses on the phonemes /ck/ and /e/ and is a red level 2 book band.